THE BOOK OF LAMENTING

ANHINGA PRESS

THE BOOK OF LAMENTING

Lory Bedikian

2010 Philip Levine
Prize for Poetry

Selected by
Brian Turner

ANHINGA PRESS
TALLAHASSEE, FLORIDA 2011

Cover art: Ephraim Rubenstein, *"Still Life with Burned Books,"*
    www.ephraimrubenstein.com
Author photograph: William Archila
Cover design: Carol Lynne Knight
Design & typesetting: Jill Runyan
Type Styles: titles set in ITC Tiepolo and text set in Garamond Premier Pro

Library of Congress Cataloging-in-Publication Data:
ISBN – 978-1-934695-26-5
Library of Congress Cataloging Card Number – 2011926683

Anhinga Press Inc. is dedicated wholly to the publication
and appreciation of fine poetry and other literary genres.

For personal orders, catalogs
and information write to:
Anhinga Press
P.O. Box 3665
Tallahassee, Florida 32315
Web site: www.anhinga.org
E-mail: info@anhinga.org

Published in the United States
by Anhinga Press
Tallahassee, Florida
First Edition, 2011

In memory of Sion Abajian

The Philip Levine Prize for Poetry

The annual competition for the Philip Levine Prize for Poetry is sponsored and administered by the M.F.A. Program in Creative writing at California State University, Fresno.

2010
Lory Bedikian
The Book of Lamenting
Selected by Brian Turner

2009
Sarah Wetzel
Bathsheba Transatlantic
Selected by Garrett Hongo

2008
Shane Seely
The Snowbound House
Selected by Dorianne Laux

2007
Neil Aitken
The Lost Country of Sight
Selected by C.G. Hanzlicek

2006
Lynn Aarti Chandhok
The View from Zero Bridge
Selected by Corrinne Clegg Hales

2005
Roxane Beth Johnson
Jubilee
Selected by Philip Levine

2002
Steven Gehrke
The Pyramids of Malpighi
Selected by Philip Levine

2001
Fleda Brown
Breathing In, Breathing Out
Selected by Philip Levine

Contents

Acknowledgments

Grateful acknowledgment is made to the editors of the following publications where some of these poems, or earlier versions of them (some under slightly different titles), first appeared:

Ararat: "Caravan"
Cold Mountain Review: "At My Mother's Dresser"
Connecticut Review: "Washing of the Feet, Lake Sevan, 1997"
Crab Orchard Review: "Night in Lebanon," "Chameleon,"
    "Two Open Palms"
Drumvoices Revue: "Murmurings"
Eclipse: "How They Appear," "Kerosene"
Euphony: "The Fishermen," "Self-Portrait with Crane"
Grist: "The Mechanic"
Harpur Palate: "On the Way to Oshagan"
Heliotrope: "Counting"
Malpaís Review: "Father Picking Grapes, Armenia, 1997"
Poet Lore: "Trance"
Poetry International: "The Brother," "The Divide"
Portland Review: "Father's Mirage," "Letter from Beirut"
Timberline: "Beyond the Mouth"
Westwind: "Bringing Nanig the News"

"Night in Lebanon" was reprinted in *Blue Arc West: An Anthology of California Poets* (Tebot Bach), in the *Levantine Review, Armenian Reporter* and was featured on the Poets Against War website. It was chosen as "Poem of the Month" by Writers At Work and received the Dr. Aram Tolegian Award in Poetry from the Armenian Allied Arts Association. "Beyond the Mouth" was reprinted in the *Armenian Reporter.* "The Brother" received an honorable mention in the Daniel Varoujan Prize from the New England Poetry Club Contests. "Prayer for My Immigrant Relatives" was a Common Prayers project winner from Writers At Work and received citywide distribution. "Proposal" won first place in the New England Poetry Club 2008 Barbara Bradley Award contest.

Thanks to Lola Koundakjian, the Armenian Poetry Project and Joshua Robbins, Little Epic Against Oblivion, for including poems and for support.

My sincere gratitude and appreciation to the Money for Women/Barbara Deming Memorial Fund for a generous grant in 2006, which made the completion of this collection possible. My thanks to Arpa Foundation for Film, Music and Art for a grant in 2008 toward the publication of this manuscript.

The Book of Lamenting was selected as a finalist for the 2007, 2008 and 2009 Crab Orchard Series in Poetry Open Competition Award, and for the 2007 and 2008 Crab Orchard Series in Poetry First Book Award, for which I am honored and grateful.

I would like to thank the University of Oregon for a Graduate Teaching Fellowship and Garrett Hongo, Dorianne Laux and Pimone Triplett of the Creative Writing Program for guiding me in the starts and revisions of several of these poems. I thank my instructors/professors at De Anza College and at the University of California, Los Angeles — especially Prof. Stephen Yenser — for my early education in poetry.

For her readings, comments and moral support, my thanks to Roxane Beth Johnson. My humble thanks to Eavan Boland and Yusef Komunyakaa for their support of my work, and to Rick Campbell and Lynne Knight of Anhinga Press who through their hard work made this book a reality. Many thanks to the students and to Prof. Connie Hales of the MFA Program at California State University, Fresno for giving these poems a chance, and immense gratitude to Brian Turner for believing in my work and choosing my manuscript.

To all those who have blessed me with friendship, thank you.

I thank my parents, Vahan and Zevart Bedikian, for their unending and unconditional care.

And my deepest gratitude to my husband, William Archila, for his own poetry, immeasurable strength, support and love.

THE BOOK OF LAMENTING

I

Beyond the Mouth

On the back of every tongue in my family
there is a dove that lives and dies.

At night when my aunts and uncles sleep
the birds comb their feathers, sharpen beaks.

They are carriers, not only of the olive
branch, but the rest of our histories, too.

As from the ark, we came in twos
with tired eyes from Lebanon, Syria,

the outskirts of Armenia, anywhere
safety said its final prayers and died.

Like every simile ever written, the doves
on our tongues are tired and misread.

Dinners begin with mounds of bread,
dialogues piled between the older men.

Near our dark throats, the quiet
birds lurk to watch meals descend,

takes phrases that didn't reach
the truth and spin them into nests.

Now and then, we spit them out in shapes
of seeds, olive pits, spines of fish.

The men never watch what enters past
their teeth, what leaves their moving lips,

and the doves know this. The women shut
their mouths when they don't approve

of the squawking laughs. There is a saying
(or at least there should be) that if one doesn't

believe what is said or true, they can ask
the dove on the back of the tongue

and it will chirp the ugliness or the pitted
truth, of how we choke on what we hide.

Night in Lebanon

The youngest boy, with his ulcer,
sleeps. His lower lip pulsates, a small fish
breathing. A bed of torn pillows, cradles four
of them, two brothers, two sisters —
curved, quiet on the living room floor.
Buzzing, the open window has its mouth full
of street lights, mosquitoes, those who stay
awake. Peeled paint on the ceiling, the door

sheds the skin it wore through
a drawn-out, civil war. The parents
sleep in a room full of faith
hammered to the walls. Posing, a copper
cross, its inscription asks in Armenian
for blessings of God upon this home.
Through the mother's sleeping lips a prayer
slips, drifts, hovers above the boy

who dreams: he's a grown man
spinning yarn around their home
until it's as thick as a bombshell.
Then, cane in hand, walking through cedar
groves, he drops his string of worry
beads into a well. Cracking a pumpkin
seed open with his teeth, he tastes
childhood in each closed casing.

In the morning, a thin scroll
of bread filled with tomato paste, oil, mint
will start the hurried day. But now, he sleeps
as he did the day he was born. Stillness
enters his lip, his mouth finally rests,

breathing as he will when he is older
than this war whose finger has carved a scar
in him, the size of an eye that will not close.

The Brother

The news comes at daybreak.
Your brother is dying.

In Beirut, the sun swells
into twilight, as electrical wires

weave deserted webs, a grocer
puts away his wooden stool,

every dirt road stands still.
Sighing into the phone,

your nephew waited all day
to tell you, paces the balcony

scented by his father's
last cigar. *It's no surprise,*

he says, *old age. We're thankful
for what war could not do.*

On a wall below, a moth
flies into a hole, footprint

left from a bomb.
Before lowering

the receiver, you tell him
I will send money soon.

Outside, the day begins, but here
the sun is hollow, here the wires

run straight as the sidewalks
below. Through the window

two boys cross the street.
You want to cry out,

make them turn around,
but instead you wait, hear

one calling to the other to slow down,
to look before he reaches the other side.

Father Picking Grapes, Armenia, 1997

We watch from the Moscovich
as he steps into the ditch,
our driver begging him to hurry.

These grapes are from Hayasdan
he says, as he steps up to the car,
plucks one for each of us.

Let the owner complain. Let him
knock me down. I have waited
my entire life to pick these grapes.

He sings a familiar, dark cluster
of notes in the dry October air.
The hills, now camels at dusk, stare

at swallows swimming above,
look to the dusty road
that meets the horizon. As if someone

approaches, he listens, almost
waits for a relation, long lost,
to walk toward this remote village,

to find him here with his palms full of harvest,
full of vines that have waited for his return.

The Fishermen

Resembling the shape of a whale from outer space,
      the Bronze Age stuck in the sediment, and fossils,
            called Gegham Sea in ancient times, now home

to gulls and geese, otters extinct, surrounded by fields
      of cemeteries, carved khachkars below oak trees
            — only some of what I've read about this place.

But none of this matters when they enter the scene:
      out of a beat-up van, with woolen caps, faces
            of dark wood, edged, knuckling cigarettes,

hair like yarn, dragging their feet, in some
      eyes a glint of copper, in others nothing.
            They are the fishermen who come to Lake Sevan,

from the province of Geghark Unik, other villages,
      and I cannot take my eyes away. I feel like a young girl
            watching stars or heroes.

Fishermen of need, not sport, they've come to hunt
      sig, goldfish, crayfish, trout, and the prince fish
            of these waters. With bait and hook,

lines and nets, they've come to cast
      into the turquoise mass, hoping to reel in
            scales and fins, rough as their unshaven beards.

I want to ask them if they're anglers, what tackle they'll use.
      I want to watch them as they clasp suspenders, yanking
            on their boots, black as tar, black as their brows.

They stagger themselves along
        the beach like bowling pins. Some turn
                to me with stares full of sand.

One of them steps out of a photo album of my childhood
        with his stubbly chin, onyx eyes, hands coarse
                as tufa, coffee-stained teeth. As he cups

his hand to light a cigarette, he smiles. I grab my camera,
        wanting to remember this, how they tug at their slickers,
                scratching their heads, looking out to the lake, hoping

for dinner or catch to sell, how I stop thinking of folklore
        and storks at the sight of them, ignore my driver
                calling to me as they turn, slip into the water's edge.

Kerosene

In winter, they wait.
The line veins
through city buildings,
ashen pillars.

A man pulls his collar up
the coat, thick, black.
A woman disappears
into her moleskin shawl.

There is nothing emptier
in this season than the tanks
by their feet, sour smell,
burnt oil rising from caps

twisted off. Young boys
watch each other, sit
on the frozen containers,
lumber along when it's time

to move a foot forward.
Soon, a hydrocarbon,
petroleum elixir will bring
flames to battered stoves.

There is nothing as quiet
as Yerevan, when people
stand waiting for fuel
rationed, yawning

through sunrise, white
clouds rising from their lips

into the sky, strata of rock,
when their coats move along,

their fingers frozen with coins.

Washing of the Feet, Lake Sevan, 1997

I rush to pass the dried, wheat-colored brush.
My city shoes are polished black and break
the brambles growing out from swollen earth.
What drives my haste to reach it, I don't know,
perhaps because I find this land of lost
geology. I seek the photographs
that never made it back, developed blank
from Grandma's camera, after her pilgrimage.
I move as one does to mirage, the mind
so quick to change what is and is not real.
As if I'm in a well kept home, I leave
my shoes and socks, walk across the pebbled bank.

This is not the sand I've known, not the life
I've led. A blotch of rocks, the size of coins,
lines the bank and dips into the water's edge.
I enter, shatter the still life, try to wash
the anger from my feet. I throw the rocks
from where I am, call out the names of lovers
gone. The voice that leaves my mouth trembles now.
I roll my pants up high and move a deeper step
into the solemn lake. The muffled light of day
is mimicking my thoughts. I try though to forget
anything before this trip, the city jobs,
the stacked boxes I move from home to home.

The liquid clear, I bend to see my hand
below the water's face. When I was nine
and heard my brothers bickering, I plunged
my hands into the fluid crust of lake,
not quiet like this one and far above the sea.
I could not tell what might come up at grabbed
sediment, terrified to think of nothing found

but dirt and sand — no sign of life to hold
up in the sun. My brothers' voices seemed
to melt into my excavation's splash.
I thought the rock thrown back within was anguish.
I claim this old lament as mine, each nail

a scar on the fingertip, each broken hair
an unforgotten word, a held-off stare.
Why have I held their tempers for them all
these years? Perhaps I've come to cleanse regret —
to grieve the battered door, the broken lamp
that never made it across the room. Step
by step, they'd lunge toward each other. How
could that child know her brothers would survive?
Perhaps that's why I've come to see what lies
just at the edge of memory. My reach
will clasp a color, a shape. Mistakes we've made
are impressions left below the surface. Each

fault speaks its own true language, fossilized code.
The blurry water saves me from too much
recalled. The dizzy ripples glide. Just like
distracted years, they let me take my time. (Tired,
I wish I could just play the tourist's part.)
Around the lake, the arid grasses lounge.
The leaves are amber stars. So, this is autumn
in Armenia. But I don't know what drew
me to this world. All I see are rocks and grains
below my feet. The herons cup their ears.
The sky has swallowed all its shades of gray,
and question marks are in the shapes of trees.

December 7, 1988

After breakfast, I made tea, sat down to drink, fold socks. Suddenly a noise like a bomb. I thought we were being attacked. Then darkness.

⌒

The air was thick with dust. I ran to the school. It looked like someone had buried the city in large mounds of rubble.

⌒

We found Avo's body the next day. His teacher, the other children were all dead. My husband, a sculptor, chiseled a piece for the cemetery. Flowers, that's what I bring. Carnations, when they're available. Sometimes I make paper flowers, the kind they used to put in the windows of the school. In the sculpture, the teacher is holding a dove, the children, their schoolbags.

⌒

I had to burn Avo's furniture to make fire. There were no trees left, here or in Gyumri.

⌒

In the mornings, I still make tea. The house still shakes. My son visits in dreams, plants trees. Sometimes we walk through Spitak, recite poems, the alphabet. With a stick, he writes his name in the earth. I wake myself up before he can scrape the letters away.

On the Way to Oshagan

I stop the car, cross the dirt road
to see what the old woman's selling.
Hoping for a cold drink, an extra
postcard to write this evening, I find
her tucked behind a table, under a tarp,
fly swatters swaying above her head.
Stacks of Marlboro boxes, packs of gum
are the only things I recognize among
the odd Russian, Armenian labels.
She must not hear me, because she keeps
rolling a square of newspaper into a cone,
fills it with roasted sunflower seeds.
I ask for one, saying "meg hahd hahjees,"
fumbling to find a *dram* among my dollars.

Her eyes, the color of two almonds
rise for only a moment before she asks
with a low, coarse, parrot-voice
if I like America, if I'm married and where
exactly is this place called "Glendale?"
With an awkward smile I drop indifferent
answers for her, like coins in the palm.
Until this exchange I had convinced myself
that I do not look like a tourist. After all, having
an ancestral name, firm family tree, the language
ironed to my tongue since the day I was born,
how could I be just another *Amerigatzi*? I say
this to myself, though I'm the one with the walking
shoes, the camera, the plaid-patterned pants.

She interrupts my thoughts with "Welcome
to Armenia. Please take these seeds for free."
When I extend the money, I notice her face

shrinks in the afternoon light. Back in Los Angeles
I would have insisted to pay. But with this unexpected
visit I simply remembered how I was raised,
before the textbooks, the corporate cubicles,
before I learned to get fashion magazine
haircuts, attend culturally sponsored events.
I hear my parents say, "Love this seven-member family
all your days and nights, learn to take every offering
with grace, no matter the given size."
I bow my head, say thank you. She insists
it's nothing, asks that I come back soon.

Forgetting why it was I stopped at all,
I walk back across the dirt, cracking
one open. Its shell tastes of the same
salted seeds tucked by my grandmother
into coat pockets for evening walks.
Like a small communion, I contemplate
the seed with my tongue and swallow.
I almost turn to wave, but get back
in the car. For miles around, there is nothing
but land I follow on the map.
There is nothing but this old woman
and her convenience stand
made of brick and wood
on the edge of a beaten road.

Levon

Cousin Levon looks like Khalil Gibran
at sixty-eight. I notice this as he drives us
around the outskirts of Beirut, toward road
blocks, looking out the windows at cattle,
dried brush, abandoned cedar trees, the rib cages

of buildings after war. What did we want to see?
The Taj Mahal of the Mediterranean —
a huge reptile skinned at the bottom of the piers?
October, 1997. My best friend entered the circle
of a wedding ring. I broke up with a magician

who made water turn to money. Could I care
any less about Lebanon? No — until my father
admitted all around he could smell the ghosts
of his parents, in the falling eucalyptus leaves.
He saw his mother's eyes pinned in his sister's,

who lost herself to embroidery, to any thread
she could find while the electricity worked,
his father's hands in his brother's knuckles
leaning on a cane, grazed by breezes
full of leftover gunpowder. Levon nods

at whatever my father says. Not one
argument between them, but stories
in Armenian, Arabic. Levon must be
my father's age, but calls my father, *Uncle.*
I don't tell Levon he resembles the bard

of Beirut, I don't even think of poetry.
Instead I wonder where the ghosts are now,
if the scent is stronger at dawn or dusk,
if they know how far we've come,
if they can hear the rumbling of our wheels.

Letter from Beirut

Dear Cousin —

The country is on fire again.
Today, rockets hit nearby.
Lebanon is so small
everything can be heard.
For years we have known
the language of bombs.
But tonight, tonight it is quiet.

The country is falling.
People have fled their homes.
Children are dead.
Here, in the eastern part,
we are safe, for now.

Sorry for writing you late.
Everything is shut down.
I have no work.
Indoors most of the time.
We sit and wait for news.
Our lights flicker on and off
like the winter moon.

People's hearts have turned
hard as rocks. No one walks
the streets. Only the old men
at the corner argue until dusk.
They are so close to death,
they don't tremble as we do.

For now, this much.
It is difficult to write.

Our ears are accustomed
to explosions and running feet.

But tonight, tonight it is so quiet,
so silent you could hear

the strike of a match.

Prayer for My Immigrant Relatives

While they wait in long lines, legs shifting,
fingers growing tired of holding handrails,
pages of paperwork, give them patience.
Help them to recall the cobalt Mediterranean
or the green valleys full of vineyards and sheep.
When people's words resemble the buzz
of beehives, help them to hear the music
of home, sung from balconies overflowing
with woven rugs and bundled vegetables.
At night, when the worry beads are held
in one palm and a cigarette lit in the other,
give them the memory of their first step
onto solid land, after much ocean, air and clouds,
remind them of the phone call back home saying,
We arrived. Yes, thank God we made it, we are here.

How They Appear

No one understands the ghosts
　　　　　we know.

They are floating hieroglyphics
　　　　　of flame.

I say to people: look further
　　　　　so you can see

their shapes, faces clear
　　　　　as thunder.

Grandmother and I sketch them
　　　　　while awake,

flashing in the midday sun
　　　　　like copper pennies.

When I leave her side, the ghosts
　　　　　drag themselves

as leaves into the subway's stairwell
　　　　　and as I work

some stay with her, braiding her hair down
　　　　　the length of our street.

I see ghosts in the ice
　　　　　of a cocktail,

see them hanging from branches
　　　　　of a willow tree.

When sounds stir in the coffee, I write
        what they creak.

How can I begin to tell disbelievers
        their names?

How can I begin to show the fear
        these ghosts know,

like the screaming crow
        flying from a hurricane?

Bringing Nanig the News

She smells of mint and lemon.
At dusk I sit with her while she hums

old country lullabies, in between sips of tea.
With one hand she holds the letter

about a sister dying in Yerevan,
while her other hand seems to grow out

of the wooden curves of her cane.
My grandmother never cursed

until this moment. She said the devil
lived in the husband who beat her sister.

I place my hand on my hip
as if to be strong for her.

But I don't know this type
of man, I don't know this type

of trouble and instead of patting
her back, I dream of the weekend ahead.

Too young, impatient, I long
for the air that sits on her porch.

Into a bible, she tucks the letter.
It is when she begins to sing

again about saints and healing
that I listen, hide my eyes

and the age of my indifference.

Lentils

Barely ten, I watch my aunt
pour the bag of raw seeds —

orange orbs spill down
to a silver tray, flat and wide.

Her fingers push pebbles
to one side, shove hair

behind her ears
as she works, bows over

the pile of grain, makes
dinner for the seven of us.

Handing me a shaker of salt,
my cue is the blink of her eye.

Her radish cheeks begin to glow
above the boiling pot. Quiet,

I watch the blackened yarn
of her brows, the dark olive

of her skin. Beauty marks,
moles map her arms.

A somber bird, a movie star —
I can't decide what she is.

Single and thin, Syrian-born,
she sorts, counts lentils.

And each day, not a word,
not a complaint through her lips,

just her hold on a wooden spoon,
apron tied tight behind her back,

stirring, stirring the boiled seeds,
always above an open flame.

At My Mother's Dresser

I lift my five-year-old
body on the chair to watch
her fingers lift blush powder,

(*burnt rose*), to her face.
The strokes seem counted
out, maybe twenty brushes

on each cheekbone. In the mirror
I mimic her, but she doesn't
smile, and instead, dabs

perfume on her wrists and neck,
combs back her stiff, chestnut
hair cut short above the ear,

a bird's nest, a crown, adjusts
an opalescent button in the silk
blouse's eye, the stockings

already torn. Without a word,
sigh, in haste she chooses
large, red, faux bijou beads

to hide the pale olive of her skin.
I know these things make her
stand apart from the others —

PTA mothers, grocery clerks,
the women in afternoon dramas.
I will grow to resemble her: our eyebrows

too dark, two brush strokes of rain
clouds, our noses edged pyramids,
always causing a double look, a glance.

She rubs cream under the eyes'
half-moons, taupe for the lids.
To match her nails (another burnt hue

of red) she fumbles for the final touch
on her mouth. She needs to hurry
before they arrive: the relatives

who have been missing for years,
names mentioned, tossed photos
in a shoebox, phone calls cut short,

people she hated to leave behind
in Syria while she and my father
made the trek to the States.

As she swirls lipstick toward her mouth,
one hand smoothes the color on
as the other dabs the crying

that's begun. She does this without a change
of face. She does this as if it's part
of dressing, of carrying on.

Covello Drive

In the suburbs, in the hot valley
of southern California, in a home
made of stucco, with clanging
dishes echoing in the hollow walls,
the days drove themselves to sleep.

The wire fences held the yards of ivy
from overgrowing, from winding themselves
around the rusted cars, fiberglass carports,
angry pit bulls, the smog in its infancy,
flies foraging rotted fruit on the pavement.

This was Van Nuys in the seventies.
And this is part of what I remember:
my father waited to see the fig tree grow,
waited to see his three children
eat dinner in peace. My brothers

shot basketballs through hoops, shouts
turned into fists and feet, an uproar,
a slamming of doors swallowed
by a street-sweeping machine.
Like tangled roots, they fought.

Something in our house always broke
behind a muffled voice: a glass, a window.
Father was always the last to know
of the bruises, the threats. His life
had turned into mornings

of worn-out nametags. Father
wondered if the other kids on our block
also split hinges in half. All night, he stared
out toward that fig tree, waited
to see what portions would grow,

wondering what would break.

The Mechanic

Stretching over the carburetor,
he shouts about the quality of life here
compared to back home, how they stood
in line for bread, how there were no cedars
more green than those by the shore.

He could be my uncle in Syria, 1948,
a man taking in fumes, a cigarette balancing
on a fender, hands lined with grease,
saving coins in a jar for his newborn,
losing relatives to malaria, to civil war.

But today we're in Hollywood — the palms
dry. This man speaks to me in Armenian.
He remembers working late into the Lebanese night,
the plaza's noise of backgammon boards,
headlights beaming beyond the Mediterranean.

Now, he's used to customers calling out
his American nickname, while he wrenches
spark plugs into place, the old country
preserved on a calendar. He's used to this
new world of dollar bills, available parts.

I say bless him and this hand-made auto shop,
the first opening, closing of hoods, pump of pistons.
And bless the one who never made it over
the Atlantic, an arm extending into the engine,
a scar exposed, the shape of an eagle's wing.

Two Open Palms

I want to know my father
so I begin to watch his hands.

They roast the almond in mid-afternoon,
shave the blemished flesh of the yellow pears

before his family returns from work.
He speaks of his mother, her hands

taught him to pare the apple. Perhaps
it's why he speaks to the McIntosh

while peeling it before bed. His stories
slice into the evening's silence.

He brings out the quince, the orange
plums to have something spin within

the mouth while he remembers her:
a woman in the middle of Lebanon,

scraping the lemon's skin to scent
the humid air, to rouse her swollen eyes.

With the chestnut's shell between his palms
he rubs these words and makes

cadences fall onto the empty plate.
He stops when he cannot go back

there anymore. Perhaps speaking of her
now is not as simple as picking

the grape from its twisted, gnarled vines.
The evening quiets, a fruitless tree.

What he cannot say, he carves
into wedges of rotted, skinned persimmon

that he throws away. I've seen those
bruises piled in the bag by his feet.

I never ask him too much. Her stories
come to me in portions, like the spring

fruit he cannot bear to overlook.
So, instead I help him gather beads

from the heart of the pomegranate.
We choose what is ripe enough to eat.

Father and I sit, make sure to discard
the seeds from the Bing cherries,

the honeydew melon and apricot.
When his grasp loosens, tires,

his fingers pause on a stem. Then for him,
for a change, I bring out bread and cheese,

and we gnaw at pits from the Kalamata
while laughing through our teeth.

The Divide

Below willow leaves,
      draped in October mist,
            my father sits.

Apricot orchards turn
      into the cedar groves
            of Lebanon,

while he opens
      his first prayer book
            to a photo weighted

with wool vests,
      with sleep that never comes
            from midnight's crickets.

A wooden table stands between
      his father — a man who worked
            the earth in clouds of dust —

and his mother — her eyes
      half-shut. They wait
            for his letters from

New Jersey, Connecticut,
      San Francisco, his trek West.
            For a sign, they read

the crow's nest
      on the woodpile,
            count the feathers

of a dead dove
        under the church's steeple.
                The day he left, they tucked

a cross in his pocket,
        sewed a blue bead
                under his collar.

He will become a minister,
        his parents' wish fulfilled
                before they are buried

by strangers, years later, a bible
        open above their graves.
                But now, the yard — without pulpit —

gives no signs in this new world.
        He kneels to pray,
                but only sees himself

turning back. On the porch,
        the table's grain
                holds them up

until he is gone.
        This is what he knows:
                the art of lamenting —

to take shapes
        lost, and plant them
                below his feet,

until his skin becomes
      the sepia of old age.
            He thinks nothing

can separate him
      from them, not even
            the thick fog rolling in.

The Car Breaks Down in Kettleman City

The back of father's head —
full of stunted curls, smoky wisps
in half-circles above his neck —

turns, looks for a mechanic, a sign.
He breaks into song, perhaps from Gomidas,
lamenting lost land, lost mountains,

but I know it's really for a brother lost to war,
for two unmarked graves of his parents
on a barren hillside, just like this one,

for the sound of his sister's teeth clicking
on a melon seed to open its dry shell,
for years of driving in tunnels of thought.

From a dirty pay phone, we call for assistance
and wait. We're quiet. The car is dead.
Here, California looks like Lebanon.

I watch him — sermons lost in his pores,
letters unwritten for decades. Father,
for once, cut your lament in half.

Save us both. Empty your pockets
of the noise you carry, of your family scattered
like spilt rice, nightmares you mumble in sleep.

Why must every tune be a darkened sky?
Why must every deserted dirt road
remind you of those back home?

He shields his eyes with palms while he waits
as if he can't bear seeing the open land,
the imposing brightness all around him.

The Book of Lamenting

begins on edges of highways

where the sun raises its swollen belly,
grasses outgrow themselves,
vineyards wither their nerves.

The sun cracks the dashboard,
slithers between rows of eucalyptus, juniper,
rolls along the wheels of trucks.

Past crows that caw, pod atop railroad crossings,
the engine cranks its monotonous pulse, distracts me
from posted signs, the yellow snake that guides me along.

This is where I find reasons to question the living,

my father's face held
in his hands, his brows etched
in the stained glass of the missions,

my mother's sacrifice dwelling
in deserted turnpikes, her eyes
gazing from overgrown orchards.

Trees disappear. Dried brush crumbles
into camel's fur. In the distance, no horizon,
but tumbleweed large as sheep.

This is where I am when the world has closed its ears,

alongside rusted tractors, abandoned fruit stands,
roaming for hours, nothing but barbed-wire fences,
nothing but the smells of harvest and gasoline.

The road matters more than the earth,
more than those on the road, it turns
into a spine, ladder of teeth and bone.

In the passenger seat, my grandmother's ghost
holds a palm full of seeds, scatters them
skyward for the crows to eat.

All of it behind us now. She tells me
not to tangle my nerves, not to stop
the creed of the open road —

nothing that runs can stay the same.

III

Desk

When the floods come
I swim to it.

From the stew
of water, my arms

loop and wheel, frantic
for that large mahogany slab.

Parachutes of waves
all around, I barely keep

afloat. This tsunami,
this ocean is full of debris.

I must have wandered
from shore again.

I glide and finally reach
its chipped edges. Glorious

boards and drawers,
my rectangular lifeboat:

I jump on its strong back,
lie down, breathe

and say, *Thank you.*
The rocking settles.

I say, *Listen, there's so much*
to tell, so much I've seen

in my wanderings.
I have been swimming for days.

Trance

At the bottom of my kitchen sink
a brushfire; all the villages are burning.

Men on horseback gaze beyond
their own destruction; other horses

have been shot. Flames rise above
their nostrils. Trees crackle.

These men, once boys — young
legs hairless against their mother's

feet — crawled and tumbled
on a floor speckled with spices.

What did they imagine when looking
beyond the window's splintered frame?

A voice must have stopped them
from the trance that could have led

to steady reigns, plows, chisels
cutting stone. Someday the mothers return

to them, on their deathbeds, weep
for their charred fingers. I see how small

they were once, standing on a wooden
stool to reach the box of matches, hidden

high enough to save them from danger.

Caravan

He might have been a traveling minstrel,
one who knew the time of day
by how a shadow drops its weight.
He might have been my husband,
a father of future desert bards.

I felt I knew him. He found me
between the strums of his mandolin
as I dropped a clay pitcher full of milk.
A burlap knapsack was his pillow,
while I slept under the arched canvas.

He drove the caravan, his dry hands
tangled with dark leather reigns,
his body a long bamboo reed
mimicking the jerks of the terrain,
burning under a midday sun.

Before we reached any sign of water,
the horses would clap their tongues
on their risen lips, above their rotting teeth,
and the man would shout at them
while the wheels complained

over pebbles, sticks and leaves.
We settled below a canopy of trees,
and he brought out the lute —
its hollowed walnut shell took him
away. By sundown, the melon shape

on his thigh took my place
as I forced a thread over a wooden
knitting needle, my lap a pool of yarn.

He could have become a priest,
a legend, if he hadn't left the lute

by the copper pot that morning
before dawn. With his knapsack strapped
on his curved back, he must have fled
quickly in a direction where sunlight
fell. He must have known

I would turn the lute into a fire.

Harvard Square

Running down the ramp, tight hold on my bag,
I collide with the kid who sets up his amp.

Before I can make it in, the T shuts its mouth.
Above ground, I had lost a good half hour

watching intellects play chess in Au Bon Pain.
I stayed until I could forget

why I moved from L.A. to Boston,
could forget the unpaid bills,

the call that said he'd lost his mind.
Someone slapped the last piece down.

The sound broke us up like an old movie cop.
Late to work once again —

in the subway's beehive, I put back on
my protective I've-got-big-brothers look.

And this is where the woman enters the scene —
cane and bag, dirtied white skirt —

like a downtown bus, she stops by my side,
says, "It's better to laugh than it is to cry.

You'll learn that over the years. I lost
my glasses this morning, my house last year."

She restarts her muttering, moves to one side
while I wonder how we fit on the flat board,

her piece and mine, how the two of us wait
for the calculated moves, checkmate our kings,

weed our way out of this dingy tunnel,
find ourselves in the burst of night.

Driveways

I never understood the appeal of it:
sofa pushed to one side of the concrete
rectangle, dented garbage cans on the other,
a pistachio-colored carport over the top.

We could hear the growl
of motorcycles as they crept back
onto sidewalks until their silver bodies
blurred and then, a tunnel of noise.

Twelve, content with a borrowed bike,
I rode up and down blocks observing
the long tongues of asphalt
or white-gray stone stretched into

the runways of our suburban bungalows.
I never made sense of parked boats
covered with blue tarps, secured
from some imaginary wind, dry,

except for the occasional sprinkler
teasing its starboard side. The way
people haggled on these stretches,
washed their oil-stained squares

clean with soap, took a smoke
on a beach chair or simply stood,
hands on hips, staring toward nothing,
thinking of a time long since passed,

baffled me. The roads deserted —
now and then a pick-up truck

buzzing by, the mailman's blue bag
flashing over the concrete's bare back.

Children used them best.
Cracks were rivers, their tricycles
trains, or the slab became an island,
a basketball court, a jungle or long-awaited

classroom. It was the same square on which
they left for college, for marriage,
for some reason — and if the reasons weren't clear,
other driveways buzzed with the possibilities.

And some families fought on them —
boxing rings with someone on the lower
corner, ready to exit to sidewalk, to car,
leaving but never for good. The one standing

on the upper side, left to garden,
pulling weeds like hair, raking as if they'd find
an X somewhere, finally revealing how to get
out of this place. Front yard abandoned,

after dusk, two headlights drag
through the dark, below plum trees.
Driveways were our altars, where we could bless
and curse what we became. I rode home,

too small to know that something
makes us want to see the world
from this vantage point, from ground hardened
over earth, blaring with noonday sun,

a dead flag under our feet, rolled out
to claim a plot of land, feeling the movement
of years upon it, hand over the eyes,
calling to the window above.

Father's Mirage

Your age, a broken camel —
    makes its way beyond
        hooded caravans —
            a threadbare sweater —

each loop unravels, the yarn
    far from its woolen pattern.
        You see your forehead
            in the weave,

read your palm
    in the camel's eye.
        At the breakfast table
            a desert appears,

the camel's guise of sandstorms
    in the coffee's swirling heat.
        Your sweater's lint
            recalls men, women

dropping to the ground, rigid
    as your mother's knitting needles.
        How can I stop the minister
            from losing his mind

in a flood of bees,
    all of them dead, falling
        with your missing parents
            covered in coffee grounds?

How can I stop you
        from writing a sermon
                of words for all
                        the bruised years?

Your sweater comes undone,
        coils back to your childhood,
                a camel ride
                        when a snake

came so close you could see
        a glint of skin,
                a spool of body
                        moving the earth below it.

I give the camel water
        and it opens one eye.
                I walk around you,
                        tug at your sleeve.

But, you don't see me.
        Instead, you count olives
                in place of coins,
                        knit your brow.

I want you to remember
        how the snake could have done it,
                eaten your sweater whole,
                        your life nothing but a desert.

Chameleon

I learned to live in the willow
but did not succeed as others did
at keeping cold-blooded ways.

My plates were made of hammered tin
and I wore them just before the wind
grew in the shape of a lion's mouth.

Blue for my brothers, the color of a bruise
learning its name, is what I became
under the arched arm of bark.

And I was a girl, I'll admit, just the same,
one who had learned to raise a palette
to the sun in the painter's pose.

Teal for the morning mint tea, yellow
to find the sour grass just below the apricot's
blooms were my robes, my pleated veils.

What was the color of that day when I turned
amber against its brow? How dark was my shade
and how deep had the fossils gone?

It is good to speak in my own tongue — not
the wrinkled olive, the guttural sigh, not
the straight-back chair of stiff sonnets,

but the mouth knowing the words behind it
move in lavender, in tangerine, in a black
so black it has taken its own wings and moved

beyond the willow's space. And why can't I speak
this way? Who cannot understand this speech?
It's as simple as my skin. It breathes in the air

and knows the temperature of hate, as it knows
gold, the perfect color of pain. The apricots knew
this color. They knew that the willow was not far

from my window. I was only the memory of green
in my grandmother's arms, in my grandmother's arms,
she knew the willow and how it became ...

What Floods the Hour

This evening, the light does not fail,
neither do the stars, my voice, bright
colors of old jazz albums. Perhaps,
my mind fails — this basin of nerves,
nebula does not utter the right words.

It looks at the damp bush against the window,
remembers *leh, leh, leh, leh seeroon loree
anousheeg loree*, the melody stuck
between a star and a membrane. Who will sing
this to me when I am old? All around me

stillness, but my mind reaches
to a moment in Armenia when Anoush told me
her husband used to beat her, and so the day
he came home with the breath of a dragon,
she pushed him into the ditch dug for grape vines,

threw in his bottles of bourbon for warmth.
Is the light failing now? I keep an inventory
of the evening: books in place, dates lost,
out of order. Something in the memory
hears my grandmother's teeth clicking

in murmurs forming the book of Luke or John,
singing hymns about God while her bed
fills itself with nightmares and ash.
Her long, gray hair becomes a rope.
My mind rattles like a toy box falling over.

Everything is a cliché — even the new bud blooming
against the glass — has been done before, the petaled
breakdown, the sob bursting like a bulb.

What doesn't seem so familiar is this:
my mind conjures up my children who wait

in the sky's nerves. I remember walking along
the Charles River picking ways to save myself
from the grips of a wedding ring. Even grandmother
dropped a pail of water and ran far into the field
when the arranged suitor came to the door.

I counted beer bottles as if they were psalms. Did Anoush
know that I too drank the stars? This evening, no, the light
does not fail, because there is no darkness in the mind.
Here, lullabies are broken records. There's always a voice
singing to me, keeping the words bottled and bright.

Crossing Out the Date

The year 1997 rose like a spiral staircase
into a ceiling of darkness.

January, full of broken glass, emergency
room bills, spun stitches like a nest

while I learned how to sob by roadsides.
March bloomed into black magnolias.

There were days I licked stamps
and placed them on my forehead

so the women from the salon
would stop guessing at my destiny.

On the sidewalks, poodles the size of ants
jumped hoops made of wedding rings.

Out of the air conditioning vents, doves streamed.
Every sound in our house was a drum.

Every cigarette he smoked was the horn of a goat.
No one knew that I counted the stairs

on the way up to the reading
so that on the way down I wouldn't miss

a step. I couldn't hear what my skin
was saying, but the year did. It cupped

its ears in May and August and painted
murals on the spine of my back.

Eliot named his cruelest month,
but what about the year? At nights,

sneaking away, I'd wear the darkest colors
hoping the year was dead, but I'd hear

its breath in my ears, its tapping foot
on my nerves and no matter where I went,

its number held me,
like a baby inside the walls of a crib.

Chance

There's something to be said of surviving accidents.
My relatives believe a blue eye shields you from an evil one.
So soon they forget how luck came and went,

but insist destiny had a hand in all of it.
Like the time my car collided on the 101.
I couldn't say how I survived this accident,

except that when my car spun circles in an argument
with the rain, something stood between that wall and me.
There's another story — when the fire station sent

word to evacuate our home, mother and I spent
an hour collecting winter coats, picture frames.
There was nothing to say. We survived it.

Sometimes grandmother speaks of when they kept
themselves hidden underneath hay, in a barn.
Soon after, they forgot how long their stomachs went

without eating. After escaping, she never wept.
In her bible, she kept the names of those she lost.
Some things were never written of her survival then,
and soon, she'll forget how the story went.

IV

Illness of Kin

Dead doves open, reopen between daybreak and dusk.
      Patterns of fish leave traces of hieroglyphics.

On every pomegranate rolls the name of a beheaded ghost
      down the driveway, down the alleys

until we no longer see them walking up: the men
      with river beards and clocks for hearts,

the women with peacock feathers for hair.
      Saturn's rings on everyone's fingers spin

a carousel, commotion of a car's sputtering engine
      in our lungs, rusted, oiled with a black of coal,

of volcanoes. Back in the motherland, full of crosses
      chiseled into mud, the sheep break their necks

for sacrifice, for the old ways of astrology and myrrh
      long before the handkerchiefs hung themselves

in trees, necks of donkeys slept by fish.
      We open, reopen our eyes, throw books in a fire

burning with mint, anise, decide which illness
      suits us, the names tied to rocks,

placed below all the hats hidden from the children,
      their brows in blindfolds. Our house, nothing

but a penny on the edge of moonlight, gleams
      in silverware, newspaper gray on a finger

dialing numbers, to seas, to cypress trees riddled
        with bullets, the desert wind always in our sleep,

because dreams bring camels, goats chewing
        on dry grass, bring hospital beds, envelopes

of faded photos, even in the mailman's ear. The family
        counts pulses, heartbeats, coins in a jar,

holds their hands on their eyes,
        which open, reopen, palms facing out.

Murmurings

With eyes shut, the doctor listens
to blood move past bones, past muscles,
into ventricles and atriums.

The stethoscope lowers, his eyes
rise as I feel the flip in my chest,
a stuttering of aorta or artery.

"You have a murmur and perhaps
the valve has prolapsed."
In the living room, I tell father

my rhythm is off. Without a pause,
he says, *My heart has always murmured.*
We have this in the family. He means:

the grumbling hearts, the malcontented
elements pushing us to be less than
what we are capable of.

In silence, we sip the dark
coffee he has brewed.
Before I can ask anything,

before I can tell him what ricochets
in me, what gurgles, he finishes
off the bottom of the muddied cup,

flips it over so that bits of grind
will float to shapes we can read.
It's fortune telling, against his beliefs,

but he does this so we won't speak,
does this while our interiors mutter
on their own. The next morning I call

the doctor for results, for what they mean.
"Good news. Just a heart murmur," he says:
"Don't worry." I lower the telephone, while

my heart skips again. A frantic mouth
in my chest, it reads shapes, it murmurs,
tells me maybe the doctor heard things

I've been trying to say all along.

Hairbreadth

Today, I pluck a grey hair
out of the blackened mass,

hold it in my palm.
It shines into itself,

looming silver, bright
as planetary threads of light.

It snakes there, could climb
my arm, coil itself to spring.

But I know it's nothing
more than shed skin,

another remnant of loss.
Staring into it, I trace

Ophelia's curl, streak of sky,
glimmer of lake, the wisp

of life in a spoon. The decay
of my aging teeth is all

here too, silver-aluminum,
tarnished ebony, almost charcoal,

almost seeing the top of water,
how it hides the middle

and bottom. I close my palm.
I can't feel it at all. It plays

the ghost. It's either a fiber
to look for, or thread to toss

away, bright as a clue,
like starlight in space.

Breathing

If only I wasn't so terrible at it,
bringing in the ominous puff of air,

letting it out as a glassblower would.
If only the breath would come easy,

the large gasp under the teal daylight,
the newborn's initiation into atmosphere.

Perhaps I had gills in another life,
flapping like fall leaves, irreversible

in the way they bring the oxygen in.
Saroyan advocated this small task,

to open the lips and suck in the sky,
encouraging the lungs to nudge the ribs.

Breathe in and out, he writes, so I try it,
inhale and exhale into the paper bag,

but my lungs hardly open as they should.
Instead CO_2 barely squeezes through —

sounds in staccato, Monk's piano keys.
At times, I bring my hair to my face

cover my eyes, leave into the dark
of day, a darkness I've always known,

where breathing has no metronome,
no voice, like the child gasping under

a table, a tree, a hand, the child wheezing
into the bright, lit oncoming night.

I'm not sure where it comes from,
my stopping, blocking of the necessary.

Amazing people call me long-winded at all.
I place my hand on my chest and begin

singing the notes I heard long, long ago.
The heaving slows just as I end the song.

Counting

It must have started with hands,
father pointing to a bent index,
my brand new ring finger, short
vowels outlining his lips to speak
numbers in his own language.

In the kitchen, my grandmother made it
a necessity, a half dozen eggs singled out
to die in a bowl of sifted flour.
She taught me the ratio of coffee to sugar.
We measured spoonfuls over the flame.

Numbers kept my mother away.
That one black arm of the living room clock
took its time to bring her home.
Each day at a different interval
I counted her steps to the door.

My mind has melted into evens and odds.
I point to everything with a number,
in English to organize, in Armenian to put things
to sleep. The doctor says it's kept me company,
this succession of word after tedious word.

But I wonder why it keeps me standing
over a shattered glass, saying *seventeen, eighteen,*
to the shards I place in a paper bag,
why I've turned it into my faith, at night
counting the murmurs of the bedroom clock.

I fear I'll run out of numbers.
So I say them slower, pace each one

to the leaves of our plum tree,
fruits rotting in the wicker bowls,
curved lines in the palm of my hand.

Remedy

I have invested in kava-kava herbs
to get to the root of my problem.

The woman in the herbal section
says it calms the mind's chatter.

I've been good at being quiet lately.
No wonder it's all gone to my head.

I wonder if all of us are the same,
trying to dodge the strange dialogues

between an intellectual side of cerebrum
and an emotional, pent-up part of cerebellum.

Cerebrum, cerebellum, kava-kava, kava-kava
has become my new chant, usually rising

in the a.m. hours when no one else would
think of such things as I do.

The noise might be something mother said
regarding my bare left ring finger.

Chatter could have stayed with me like dust
in an unreachable crack of medulla oblongata.

Perhaps kava-kava will dig up a part of me
that was told to sit on her hands and not

move a budge, not even an inch, to *wipe
that smile off your face and forget about it*

what it was that made you run so fast and fall
on grass until the sky made faces back at you

and I'll only say it one more time, wipe that look
right off your face and get that idea out of your head

the one that makes you shine so bright, makes circles
of pink below your eyes and makes the rest of us so

afraid of God and whatever it is you mumble in dreams,
what you chanted years and years and years ago.

Proposal

Marry me before there is more death
in this world, before those we love

turn to ash. Each year, the trees grow
older. Each year, I believe the branches

will be full of bells and veils.
I have bent trumpets into rings,

folded sonnets into doves.
Don't say we'll wait

for an autumn of amber leaves.
It may not come. Don't tell me

I look the way I did the day
my eyes closed with wine. I see my face

in the weathered sky. Marry me
before we become the dry bark

and leaves of those decrepit trees,
faithless that a winter rain will come.

Outpatient

The spinal fluid
brings lucidity
to the small white flakes
Mihoko has found
(the neurologist)

in dark corners of
my overfed brain.
Like a blooming star,
one lesion falls on
the end of a nerve

scathing its small arm.
Clever little ball —
this causes the twitch
stuck perfectly in
my swollen left eye.

Certainly I ask,
Is this scar tissue?
Or are these years, names
pushing their way back
to a blemished skull?

Answers form like crumbs.
Pharmaceuticals
tuck me in at dawn.
Perhaps it's the dust,
embryonic junk

left from my mother's
round, dark, ticking womb.
Words have gathered like
a palm full of bees.
I can hear them hum.

Deciphering

Tonight, I'm so tired
I feel my body weep.
It speaks to itself,

avoiding dialogue, hums
cryptic messages in the dark.
I overhear deep notes, quivering

trills, almost words, but more
like the tongue praying
for itself, making a divine

liturgy for the cells.
Curves of question marks
collide in my marrow, swim

in my spine, rise to my pores.
Like old rivers, lines
in my palms crease into

a cursive I can decipher:
your grandmother once
blushed on her marriage bed;

your father has doubted
God before on a paved road
during a storm of hail;

and your mother has thought
of leaving you all, changing
her name to something

sweeter. I begin to keep a log
of symptoms: leg falling into trances,
heart's valve lagging behind.

Tonight, I discover the body laments
within its chassis, opens broken nerves
into a creed, waiting to be closed.

Prayer in the Back of the Mind

There must have been a reason
for sliding into a scream,
for navigating the hood
into just enough of a crumpled fist.

The rain slanted just before
the old four-door spiraled,
hydroplaned its gray skull.

For the steering wheel
stuck between a concrete wall
and my body, I am grateful.

And there must have been a reason
when my eyes puckered up
and pulled the nerves along
my face into harps.

I have faith in the strange
small scars that speak
to cerebrum, cerebellum,
that show how lament is marked
like scratches on a battered door.

Help my cells chant
their liturgy again.
Help the buckled ride
into a tunnel of light
to see what my body grieves
so I may stop spinning
through this hum.

I am grateful for
this neurological mess
made of rain and nerves.
May it conjure up an answer
thick as a metal chassis,
may it give me a reason
clear as a downpour of light.

Self-Portrait with Crane

On road trips, no coastal fog rolling in
brings me the sea gull or sandpiper

shifting from water to sky,
but the common Armenian crane

who treks across the Atlantic,
breaks through California clouds,

haunts the laurels, the eucalyptus,
a message tucked in its beak.

In riffs strummed on midwestern guitars,
I can hear the duduk hound me

with its drone of apricot wood,
piping a monotone dirge, driven

like the tumbleweed. In New Mexico,
each flute player's eye turns

into the pomegranate seed.
Going east should bring foliage

but I see the blue eye in trees.
For days, New England's sediment

drops into riverbeds, bends
into Gorky's brush strokes.

No relief. Ghosts float west
from Ellis Island, crosses tattooed

on their forearms, worry beads
pebbled in their grip. Even as I watch

the World Series, a fly ball
turns into the crane.

About the Author

Lory Bedikian received her BA from UCLA with an emphasis in Creative Writing, Poetry, where she was twice nominated for the Ina Coolbrith Memorial Prize in Poetry. She earned her MFA in Poetry from the University of Oregon, where she received the Dan Kimble First Year Teaching Award for Poetry. Her manuscript was selected several times as a finalist for the Crab Orchard Series in Poetry Open Competition Award and the Crab Orchard Series in Poetry First Book Award. She has received grants from the Money for Women/Barbara Deming Memorial Fund and from the Arpa Film Foundation for Music & Art. Her poems have been published in the *Connecticut Review, Portland Review, Poetry International, Poet Lore* and *Heliotrope* among other journals and have been included in *Blue Arc West: An Anthology of California Poets*. Poets & Writers chose her work as a finalist for the 2010 California Writers Exchange Award. She teaches poetry workshops in Los Angeles, where she lives with her husband. *The Book of Lamenting* is her first book.